To our parents, and parents everywhere
who raise children to love learning

Published by LONGSTREET PRESS, INC.,
a subsidiary of Cox Newspapers,
a division of Cox Enterprises, Inc.
2140 Newmarket Parkway
Suite 118
Marietta, Georgia 30067

Printed in the United States of America

1st printing, 1994

Library of Congress Catalog Number

ISBN: 1-56352-167-9

This book was printed by Arcata Graphics, Kingsport, Tennessee

Jacket and book design by Jill Dible

If I Lived In France . . .

By Rosanne Knorr
Illustrated by John Knorr

LONGSTREET PRESS, INC.
Atlanta, Georgia

We invite you to imagine
That you're a French child.
Try the speech and the customs
Of France for awhile!

If I lived in France,
Dawn to dusk every day,
The words that I'd speak
Would all be *français*.

French word:	Sounds like. . .	And it means. . .
français	frahn-say	French
bonjour	bohn-jur	hello/good day
ca va?	sah vah	how goes it?
ca va bien	sah vah be-n	it's good

When I called mom and dad,
I know they'd be there,
But they'd only respond,
If I called *mère* and *père*!

French word:	Sounds like. . .	And it means. . .
mère	may-r	mother
père	pay-r	father

Breakfast is small,
Or *petit*, as I'd say,
A *petit dejeuner*
Would start off my day.

Jus d'orange and a roll,
With hot *chocolat* and jam,
But almost never like here
With fried eggs and ham.

French word:	**Sounds like. . .**	**And it means. . .**
jus d'orange	joos door-ahn-ge	orange juice
chocolat	shaw-ko-laht	chocolate
lait	lay	milk

In France, just like here,
Learning plays a big role,
So I'd study five days
At my school, *mon école*.

French word:	Sounds like. . .	And it means. . .
mon école	mohn eh-coal	my school

Monday through Saturday,
I work at my best,
But Wednesday I play.
That's my day of rest.

French word:	Sounds like. . .	And it means. . .	French word:	Sounds like. . .	And it means. . .
lundi	loon-dee	monday	vendredi	van-druh-dee	friday
mardi	mar-dee	tuesday	samedi	sah-muh-dee	saturday
mercredi	mare-cruh-dee	wednesday	dimanche	dee-mahn-juh	sunday
jeudi	joo-dee	thursday	pas d'école	pah day-coal	no school

"*Bonjour, professeur*"
I greet in the morning.
When I leave, from afar
I yell "*au revoir*."

French word:	Sounds like. . .	And it means. . .
bonjour	bohn-jur	hello/good day
professeur	pro-fess-ur	teacher
au revoir	o-rev-wahr	goodbye

I sit quietly at a desk,
My teacher insists.
I study *six* subjects
From a long list.

French word:	Sounds like. . .	And it means. . .
combien	comb-be-n	how many
un	uhn	one
deux	duh	two
trois	twa	three
quatre	cot-ruh	four
cinq	saynk	five

Combien? How many?
Un, deux, trois, quatre,
That's one, two, three, four.
For six, add another deux more.

French word:	Sounds like. . .	And it means. . .
six	sees	six
sept	set	seven
huit	wheat	eight
neuf	nuf	nine
dix	dees	ten

Whatever I wrote,
If I made *les fautes*,
You'd hear a small moan.
"*Ah, non!* I must erase *mon crayon.*"

French word:	Sounds like. . .	And it means. . .
les fautes	lay foh-t	mistakes
mon crayon	mohn cray-own	my pencil
non	noh	no

At recess from class,
We'd run and we'd play
Up the playground and down,
At games we'd *jouer*.

French word:	Sounds like. . .	And it means. . .
jouer	jew-eh	to play

My favorite is soccer,
Called *le football* in France,
Oui, but whatever its name,
It's the very same game.

French word:	Sounds like. . .	And it means. . .
le football	luh phoot-ball	soccer
oui	whee	yes

"*Passe le ballon*,"
I tell *mon ami*.
Zut!
He tripped on a stone
And fell on his knee!

French word:	Sounds like. . .	And it means. . .
passe le ballon	pahse luh bah-loan	pass the ball
mon ami	moan ah-me	my friend
zut!	zoot	oops!

We take a small trip
By walk or subway,
So the whole class can visit
A famous *musée*.

French word:	Sounds like. . .	And it means. . .
musée	mus-eh	museum

We study the "Mona Lisa,"
La femme with the secret smile.

In that calm and quiet style.

French word:	Sounds like. . .	And it means. . .
la femme	lah fahm	the woman

If I lived in France,
A big part of each meal,
Would be bread from the bakery
Found in every French *ville*.

French word:	Sounds like. . .	And it means. . .
ville	veel	city
la baguette	lah bah-get	the long loaf of bread

When I'm close I can tell,
By the rich, buttery smell.
'Round the corner I see
The sign, "*Boulangerie*."

French word:	**Sounds like...**	**And it means...**
boulangerie	boo-lahn-jer-ee	bakery

As I enter the door,
I'm always polite.
"*Bonjour, Madame*," I say.
"Have a very good day!"

French word:	Sounds like...	And it means...
bonjour	bohn-jur	hello/good day
madame	mah-dah-m	lady

I choose a fresh roll,
All flaky and brown,
A *croissant* makes the curve
Of a smile — or a frown.

French word:	Sounds like. . .	And it means. . .
croissant	kwa-sohn	crescent roll

If I lived in France
I wouldn't just walk
I'd *me promener*
And have time for a talk.

BATEAU SUR LA SEINE!

French word:	Sounds like. . .	And it means. . .
me promener	muh pro-men-eh	to take a walk
bateau sur la Seine	bah-toh soor lah Sen	boat on the Seine

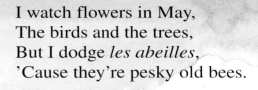

I watch flowers in May,
The birds and the trees,
But I dodge *les abeilles*,
'Cause they're pesky old bees.

French word:	Sounds like. . .	And it means. . .
les abeilles	lays ah-bay	bees

At the market, I see
Les légumes and *fruits*
I always choose some
Of my favorite, *la pomme*.

French word:	Sounds like...	And it means...
les légumes	lay lay-goo-m	vegetables
fruits	froo-ee	fruits
la pomme	lah puhm	apple

I pay in a money —
Not dollars, but *francs*,
The clerk tells me "*merci*,"
"*Merci*," is my thanks.

French word:	Sounds like. . .	And it means. . .
francs	frahnk	French money
merci	mare-see	thank you

Tout le monde, everyone,
Loves *les fleurs* same as me.
They're found everywhere.
Les fleurs are *jolies*.

French word:	Sounds like...	And it means...
tout le monde	too luh mawn-d	everyone
les fleurs	lay flur	flowers
jolies	jo-lee	pretty

If I lived in France,
I'd sit or I'd stand
With the faucet in hand
While taking *mon bain*.

French word:
mon bain

Sounds like. . .
mohn baahn

And it means. . .
my bath

Je me lave with the soap,
Til I'm clean as a whistle,
Then I brush all *mes dents*
And in *mon lit* I do nestle.

French word:	Sounds like. . .	And it means. . .
je me lave	Juh muh lah-v	I wash
mes dents	may dah-nt	my teeth
mon lit	mohn lee	my bed

I'd kiss *mes parents*
"*Bonne nuit,*" I would say,
If I lived in France
At the end of the day!

French word:	Sounds like. . .	And it means. . .
mes parents	may par-ahnt	my parents
bonne nuit	bun nwee	good night

Like a stranger on tour,
We sometimes sightsee.
Beneath *la Tour Eiffel*,
Lies the whole of *Paris*.

French word:	Sounds like. . .	And it means. . .
la Tour Eiffel	lah tour i-fell	the Eiffel Tower
Paris	Pah-ree	Paris

Then in August we're off,
Throughout the French nation,
Les vacances is a treat
A whole month's vacation!

French word:	Sounds like. . .	And it means. . .	French word:	Sounds like. . .	And it means. . .
les vacances	lay vah-kawns	vacation	mai	may	may
janvier	jahn-v-eh	january	juin	jwan	june
février	fey-vree-eh	february	juillet	jwee-eh	july
mars	mars	march	août	oat	august
avril	ah-vreel	april			

On a *train à grand vitesse*
We begin our month's recess.
Speeding fast through the night,
La ville's soon out of sight.

French word:	Sounds like. . .	And it means. . .
train à grand vitesse	treh-n ah grahn vee-tess	fast speed train
la ville	lah veel	city
septembre	set-om-bruh	september
octobre	oct-oh-bruh	october
novembre	nov-om-bruh	november
décembre	day-sawm-bruh	december

We stay at the sea
And as long as I please,
I play on *la plage*
With crowds of *amis*.

French word:	Sounds like. . .	And it means. . .
la plage	lah plah-j	beach
amis	ah-mee	friends

Now it's time to go home.
But as far as I'd roam,
If I lived in France
I'd call France *ma maison*.

French word:	Sounds like...	And it means...
ma maison	mah may-zone	my home

Rosanne Knorr has won numerous creative awards and operates
an advertising business in Atlanta, Georgia. **John Knorr** specializes
in humorous illustration for advertising and editorial publications.
Their previous book, *Atlanta: Welcome,* is captioned in five
languages. *If I Lived in France* is part of a series introducing
children to the language and customs of other countries.